ORIOLE PARK BRANCH

DATE DUE   3-30

NOV 0 8 2003			
DEC 0 2 2003			
OCT 2 6 2004			
APR - 9 2005			
DEC 1 3 2005			

DEMCO 38-296

EXPERIMENTS WITH SOLIDS, LIQUIDS, AND GASES,

A TRUE BOOK

by

Salvatore Tocci

Children's Press®
A Division of Scholastic Inc.

New York Toronto London Auckland Sydney
Mexico City New Delhi Hong Kong
Danbury, Connecticut

This young scientist
is experimenting
with liquids.

Reading Consultants
Jeanne Clidas
Rigby Education, Danbury, CT

Nanci Vargus
Primary Multiage Teacher
Decatur Township Schools
Indianapolis, Indiana

Science Consultants
Robert Gardner
Salisbury Schools
Salisbury, CT

Kevin Beardmore
Indiana Dept. of Education

**The author and publisher are
not responsible for injuries or
accidents that occur during or
from any experiments.
Experiments should be conducted
in the presence of or with the
help of an adult. Any instructions
of the experiments that require
the use of sharp, hot, or other
unsafe items should be
conducted by or with the
help of an adult.**

Library of Congress Cataloging-in-Publication Data

Tocci, Salvatore.
    Experiments with solids, liquids, and gases / by Salvatore Tocci.
       p.   cm. — (A true book)
    Includes bibliographical references and index.
    ISBN 0-516-22249-X   (lib. bdg.)   0-516-27352-3 (pbk.)
    1. Matter—properties—Experiments—Juvenile literature. [1. Solids—
Experiments. 2. Liquids—Experiments. 3. Gases—Experiments.
4. Experiments.] I. Title II. Series.

QC173.36.T63 2001
507'.8—dc21   00-052328

Contents

Now you can make things disappear just like this magician.

How Can Something Disappear?

Have you ever wanted to make something disappear? Perhaps you got the idea by watching a magician perform a trick. The magician may have put a coin in his hand. After closing his hand, waving a magic wand, and saying

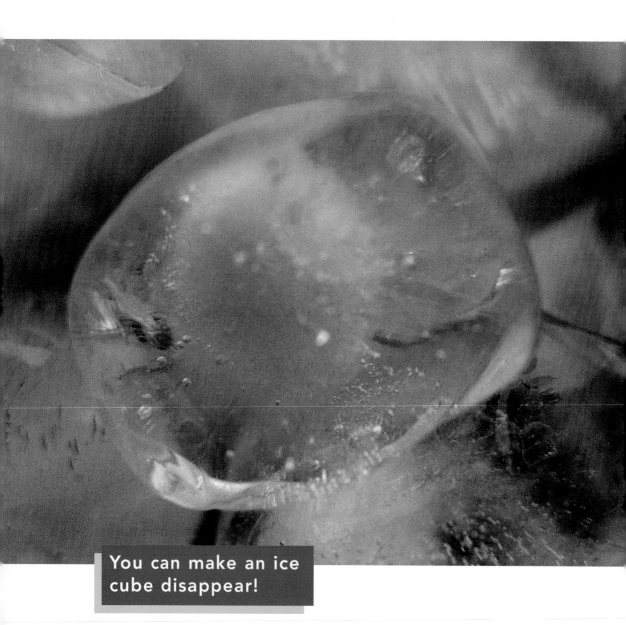

You can make an ice
cube disappear!

a few magic words, the coin disappeared.

Without practice, you could not do that magic trick easily. But there is a similar magic trick you could do right now. All you have to do is place an ice cube in an empty glass and watch what happens. The ice cube will slowly melt and turn into water. If you leave the water in the glass long enough, eventually it will be gone. Like the coin in the magician's trick, the ice cube will disappear.

However, in neither of the magic tricks did the object actually disappear. The magician uses a method called sleight of hand that made the coin seem to disappear. The ice cube melted and changed into water because of the warm air in the room. The water also evaporated because of the warm air, where it seemed to disappear. But the ice cube only changed from a solid into a liquid and then into a gas.

What Is a Solid?

Look around you. Almost all the objects that you see are solids. These solids might include the chair you are sitting on, this book you are reading, or an ice cube in a glass of soda you may be drinking. A solid is something that has a fixed shape and a fixed volume. A fixed shape

The shape of a solid, like this chair, does not change.

means that the shape of a solid does not change.

Volume is the space that something takes up. Like its shape, the volume of a solid does not change. You can tell the shape of a solid simply by looking at it. However, how can you tell what the volume of a solid is?

Solids such as a baseball and books also have fixed volumes.

Experiment 1

Measuring the Volume

You will need:
- large measuring cup
- rock

Fill the measuring cup halfway with water. Look at the numbers on the measuring cup. These numbers tell you the volume of what is in the cup. The numbers may measure volume in ounces or milliliters.

Write down the volume of water you poured into the measuring cup.

Next, gently lower a rock into the water. Write down the volume that is now in the cup. Look at both volumes you wrote down. You will see that the second volume is larger than the first volume.

Lower the rock into the water.

The second volume is larger because you added the rock. The volume of the rock adds to the volume of the water. You can figure out what the volume of the rock is.

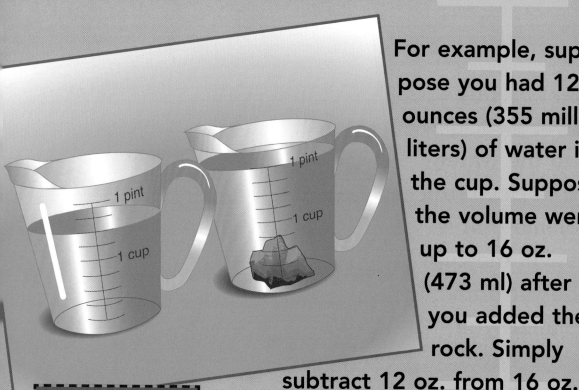

For example, suppose you had 12 ounces (355 milliliters) of water in the cup. Suppose the volume went up to 16 oz. (473 ml) after you added the rock. Simply subtract 12 oz. from 16 oz.

The volume of water has gone from 12 oz. to 16 oz.

16 oz. (volume after the rock is placed in the measuring cup)

−12 oz. (volume before the rock is placed in the measuring cup)

4 oz. (volume of the rock)

The volume went up by 4 ounces because of the rock. The volume of the rock then is 4 ounces. By the way, the water in this example has a volume of 12 ounces. Liquids, like solids, have a fixed volume. Then how are liquids different from solids?

What Is a Liquid?

Think about the water you poured into the measuring cup. Suppose you poured this water into a glass. The volume *amount* of the water would be the same as it was in the cup. In fact, the volume will always be the same, no matter what you use to hold the water.

Water is a liquid because it has a fixed volume yet can change its shape.

However, the water in the glass does not have the same shape that it had in the measuring cup. A liquid always takes the shape of the container it is in. A liquid then is something that has a fixed volume but can change its shape. Why can a liquid, but not a solid, change its shape?

Imagine that you could look very closely inside a solid with a powerful microscope. What you would see are the tiny bits or particles that make up the solid. You would also see that the particles in a solid do not move from one place to another. Because its particles stay in place, a solid keeps its shape.

Students who stay in their seats are like the particles that stay in their place in a solid.

Think of the particles in a solid as a classroom full of students sitting at their desks. The students have been told to stay in their seats and not move their desks. The students then are like particles in a solid.

Now imagine that you could peer deep inside a liquid. You would see that the particles that make up a liquid do not remain in their places. Rather, they move around freely. This is why a liquid can change its shape.

Again think of the particles in a liquid as a classroom full of students. This time, however, the students can change their seats and move their desks around the classroom.

The particles in a liquid move like students who are always moving around in their classroom.

How can you prove that the particles in a liquid move like students who change their seats?

Comparing Liquids to Solids

You will need:
- two large drinking glasses
- dirt
- stirring spoon
- several books
- cotton cloth such as a dish towel

Fill a glass halfway with water. Add some dirt and stir to make the water muddy. Place a small pile of books on a table and put the glass on top of the books. Now place an empty glass on the table. Dip one end of a cotton cloth into the muddy water and put the other end inside the empty glass. Then leave everything alone overnight to see what happens.

One end of the cloth goes to the muddy water, the other goes inside the empty glass.

The next day you should see dirt in the glass on the books. This happened because the particles of solid dirt stayed in the glass. You should also see that the cloth is wet and that clean water is in the glass on the table. This happened because the particles of water moved from the glass on the books, through the cloth, and down into the clean glass. The particles in the liquid moved from one place to another. In other words, the particles in a liquid can flow. The particles in the water all flowed at the same speed. Do the particles in different liquids, however, all flow at the same speed?

The dirt stayed in the glass on the books and there is water in the glass on the table.

Measuring the Flow

You will need:
- pencil
- two plastic cups
- watch or clock
- vegetable oil
- large bowl
- maple syrup

Use the pencil to make a hole in the side of each cup near the bottom. Place your finger over the hole of one cup. Fill the cup with water. Hold the cup over the sink and remove your finger from the hole. Time how long it takes for all the water to flow out.

Hold your finger over the hole while filling the cup with water.

Place a bowl in the sink to catch the oil.

Next fill the cup with vegetable oil. Don't forget to first place your finger over the hole! Place a clean bowl in the sink to catch the oil when you remove your finger.

How long does it take for the oil to flow out of the cup?

Fill the second cup with maple syrup. Use a clean bowl to collect the liquid. Time how long it takes for all the syrup to flow out of the cup. Which of the three liquids (water, oil, maple syrup) flows the slowest? Is there a way to make the particles of a liquid flow faster?

Speeding Up the Flow

You will need:
- two small drinking glasses
- food coloring
- clock

Fill one glass with cold water and the other glass with very warm water. Add three drops of food coloring to each glass. Notice that the food coloring flows, or slowly spreads out, through the water. Time how long it takes for the food coloring to spread completely through the water in each glass.

You should find that the food coloring spreads out faster in warm water. Heat from the warm water makes liquid particles flow faster. Because the liquid particles flow faster, it takes less time for the water and food coloring to completely mix. The warmer the water, the faster the food coloring will spread out.

Anytime you want to move faster, you need more energy. Heat provides the energy to make the particles in a liquid flow faster. What else can heat energy do besides making liquid particles flow faster?

Experiment 5

Making a Liquid

You will need:
- two identical glasses
- ice cubes
- two thermometers
- pencil
- paper
- lamp with incandescent light bulb (optional)

Fill one glass halfway with water. Half fill the other glass with ice cubes. Place a thermometer in each glass. Write down the temperature of the water and ice cubes. Place both glasses near a window so that they are exposed to the heat from the sun.

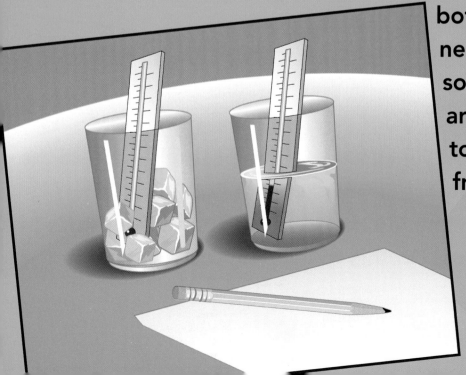

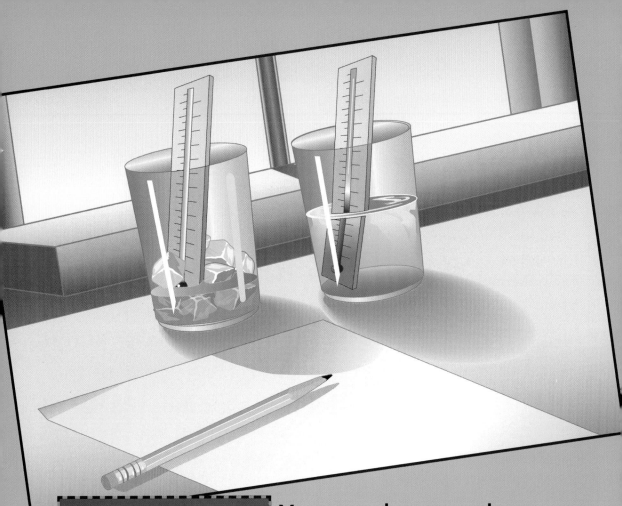

Keep both glasses the same distance away from the light.

You can also use a lamp as a source of heat. If you do, be sure that both glasses are the same distance away from the light.

Every minute, write down the temperature in each glass. Do this for 10 minutes. Notice that the temperature of the water rises. Heat energy raises the temperature of the water. Notice also that the temperature of the ice cubes does not go up as they melt. Why doesn't heat energy raise the temperature of the melting ice cubes? In this case, heat energy made the particles in the solid ice cubes move back and forth faster. The particles gained so much energy from the heat that they could also begin moving from one place to another. In other words, heat energy caused the particles in the solid ice cubes to begin acting like the particles in a liquid.

Now you know that heat energy can turn a solid into a liquid. Can heat energy also turn a liquid into a gas?

What Is a Gas?

When a solid ice cube melts in a glass, you get liquid water. When you leave the water in the glass, the water will eventually disappear. Heat energy from the warm air makes the water particles move farther away from each other. Each water particle gets far enough

Steam coming from a pot is a gas called water vapor.

away from the other water particles so that it can escape into the air. Eventually, all the water particles change into gas particles. Most people call these particles steam. Scientists call them water vapor. Water vapor is a gas.

A gas is something that does not have either a fixed shape or a fixed volume. Do gases share anything with both solids and liquids?

Experiment 6

Blowing Up a Balloon

You will need:
- balloon
- empty soft drink bottle

Blow up the balloon. Air from your lungs fills up the balloon. Now let the air out and put the balloon in an empty soft drink bottle. Turn the open end of the balloon over the rim of the bottle. Hold the mouth of the bottle to your lips. Try to blow up the balloon.

Put the balloon inside the bottle.

No matter how hard you try, you cannot blow up the balloon. Why is that? To blow up the balloon, you must fill it with air. Air is made of gases, including oxygen. But the bottle is already filled with air. Air, like all gases, takes up space. The air in the bottle takes up space and prevents the balloon from expanding.

The balloon cannot get bigger because the air inside the bottle takes up so much space.

Solids, liquids, and gases have one thing in common: they all take up space. In other words, solids, liquids, and gases all have volume. As you know, the volume of a solid or liquid does not change. However, the volume of a gas can change. How can you change the volume of a gas?

Changing the Volume

You will need:
- round balloon
- string
- masking tape
- freezer

Blow up a balloon all the way and tie it tightly. Put tape around the balloon. Place the balloon in the freezer overnight.

Make sure the tape is snug against the balloon.

36

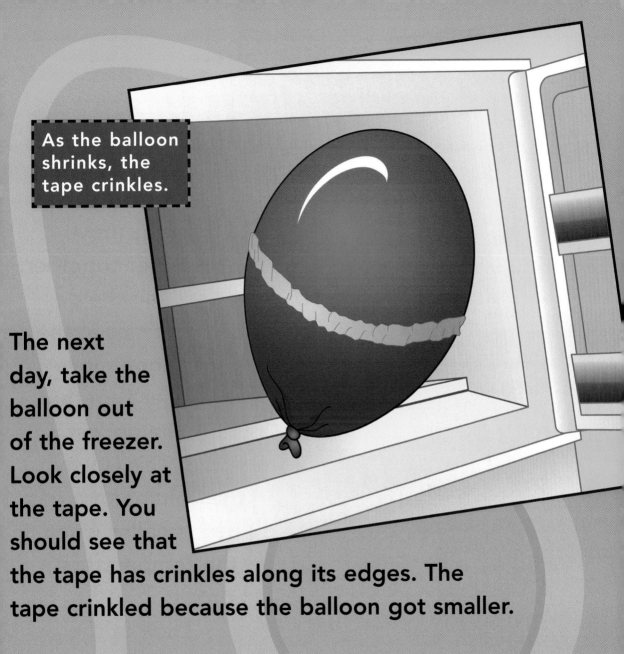

As the balloon shrinks, the tape crinkles.

The next day, take the balloon out of the freezer. Look closely at the tape. You should see that the tape has crinkles along its edges. The tape crinkled because the balloon got smaller.

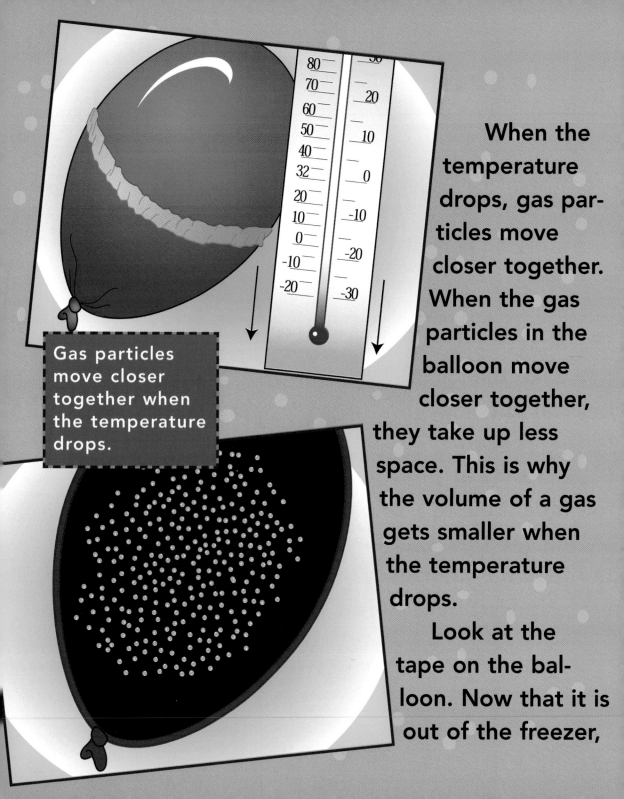

When the temperature drops, gas particles move closer together. When the gas particles in the balloon move closer together, they take up less space. This is why the volume of a gas gets smaller when the temperature drops.

Look at the tape on the balloon. Now that it is out of the freezer,

Gas particles move closer together when the temperature drops.

the crinkles in the tape should start straightening out. As the balloon warms up, it gets larger and stretches the tape.

As the temperature goes up, gas particles move farther apart. When the gas particles in the balloon move farther apart, they take up more space. This is why the volume of a gas gets larger when the temperature goes up.

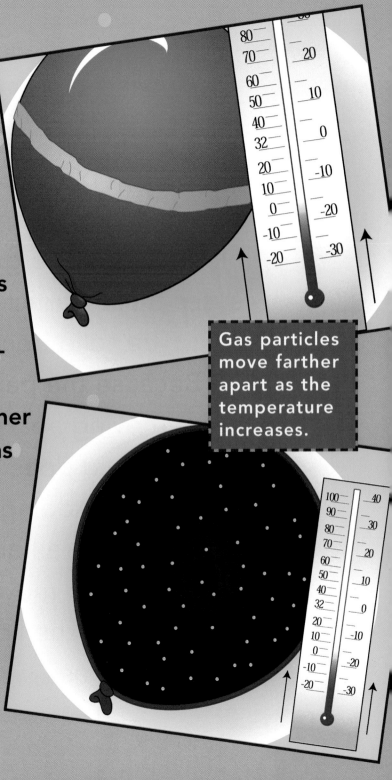

Gas particles move farther apart as the temperature increases.

The particles that make up a solid stay in place. So a solid has a fixed shape and a fixed volume. Heat energy, however, causes these particles to move apart. The solid becomes a liquid. Because the particles are always moving apart from each other, a liquid does not have a fixed shape. Adding even more heat energy to a liquid causes the particles to move even farther apart. The liquid now turns into a gas.

Fun With Solids, Liquids, and Gases

Now that you've learned something about solids, liquids, and gases, here's a fun experiment to do. See how a gas can cause a solid to "dance" in a liquid.

Dancing Raisins

You will need:
- drinking glass
- seltzer water
- raisins

Fill the glass with seltzer water. Gently drop six raisins into the glass and watch what happens. The raisins will slowly sink to the bottom. Then they will slowly rise. Once they reach the top, they will again sink to the bottom. How long do the raisins continue to rise and sink?

Why did the raisins keep sinking and rising in the seltzer water? At the top, the raisins, like most solids, sink in a liquid. But seltzer water is not only a liquid. It also contains a gas. Because of this gas, seltzer water has tiny bubbles that rise to the surface when you open the can or bottle. These tiny gas bubbles

The six dancing raisins.

stick to the raisins
after they sink to the bottom
of the glass. The gas bubbles then lift the
raisins to the top. At the surface of the
water, the gas bubbles burst. The raisins
then sink, only to rise again when more
gas bubbles stick to them.

To Find Out More

If you would like to learn more about solids, liquids, and gases, check out these additional resources.

 **Books**

Fiarotta, Noel, and Phyllis Fiarotta. **Great Experiments with Water.** Sterling Paper, 1997.

Hewitt, Sally. **Solid, Liquid, or Gas?** Children's Press, 1998.

Wick, Walter. **A Drop of Water.** Scholastic, 1997.

Zoehfeld, Kathleen. **What Is the World Made Of?** Harper Collins, 1998.

Organizations and Online Sites

United States Environmental Protection Agency
Ariel Rios Building
1200 Pennsylvania Avenue, N.W.
Washington, DC 20460
202-260-2090
http://www.epa/gov/

Click the "Kids" button and you will be led to the "Explorer's Club." Here you can click on the "Garbage & Recycling" button to learn how solids that we throw out as garbage are a serious threat to our environment.

Chem4Kids
http://chem4kids.com/

Click the "Matter" button and you will get information about solids, liquids, and gases. Some of the information has been covered in this book. However, this site can give you more information about the "three states of matter."

The National Science and Technology Center
King Edward Terrace
Parks, Canberra
Australia
http://www.questacon.edu.au/kids_home.html

This site contains games, puzzles, and fun science activities for children.

Important Words

energy ability to do work, like changing a solid into a liquid

gas anything that can change its shape and volume

liquid anything that cannot change its volume but can change its shape

oxygen a colorless, odorless, and tasteless gas that is needed for animals and plants to live

particle a very small piece or amount

solid anything that cannot change its shape or volume

volume space that something takes up

water vapor gas commonly called steam

Index

Meet the Author

Salvatore Tocci is a science writer who lives in East Hampton, New York, with his wife, Patti. He was a high school biology and chemistry teacher for almost 30 years. As a teacher, he always encouraged his students to do experiments to learn about science. When he is not writing, he spends time in the fall casting his fishing line through the air into the ocean water hoping to get a solid strike.

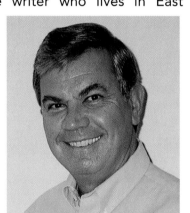